Cigarette Shenanigans; A Mixed Bag Diagnosis.

Maurie Momento

BookLeaf Publishing

Cigarette Shenanigans; A Mixed Bag
Diagnosis. © 2022 Maurie Momento

Presentation by *BookLeaf Publishing*

Web: www.bookleafpub.com

E-mail: info@bookleafpub.com

ISBN: 978-93-95784-27-6

First edition 2022

DEDICATION

To Louis, Noss and Winston,

The beautiful fur baby mans,

And to my best friends

Charlie,

Kira,

Snowball,

Sam

ACKNOWLEDGEMENT

Blame it on my ADD

PREFACE

All work throughout this book was written or edited from previous workings on a strict deadline.

Some texts contain themes related to mental health. These should be viewed through the lens of artistic expression and are not necessarily reflective of a healthy perspective.

If you are struggling with mental health please, reach out to a loved one or call lifeline on 13 11 14.

AD-LATE-D

I took a challenge to write some poems,
a new one every day,
but every time I sat to write,
my mind forgot the way,
and every time I had the energy,
the motivation wouldn't stay.

So instead of writing 21 times,
over the course of three short weeks,
I'll be writing these in 21 hours.
All at once,

Just like everything.

The CEO of Dysfunction

2

I fell.
That floor:
A mess,
Pathetic.

Undressed,
Myself,
And said:
'Forget it.'

Then lost,
That shirt,
For four
whole weeks.

Untill,
I found it,
On the floor,
Twisted,
'round my feet.

Not Nothing.

Metaphoric,
Dark.
Disdain for the present for
Aggregating the past.
A memory,
A feeling,
Fleeting and worthless,
Sinks into nothing;
To speak is superfluous -
and a little bit sad,
When words don't mean nothing,
But have already, been said.

Sell your investment property and quit profiting off the vulnerable, you capitalist pigs..

My bipolars actin' up,
Or maybe it's my ADD,
If I even have these things,
Shit, maybe I'm just fucking weak.
Better go and ask my psych -
Ok, he said:
"That will be four hundred please."
Maybe I'll just cry in bed -
At least that shit is fuckin' free..

2.

When uncertain steps form twining paths,
Sacrifice becomes an art.

RSD vs. New Thing

No, I know I'm not perfect.
I know I'm not even good,
Haven't got the timing,
But I'll keep on trying,
I'll start counting out the beats,
I'll keep on practising,
Until I find new ways to think about it,
And then one day,
I'll get better.
\\\

But my mind tells me its a day too late,
And an effort too little.
I have nothing.

Why does this empty feeling burn so deep?
I want to replace it with physical pain,
But I am an adult now, I am an adult now,
I am an adult now, I am an adult.

Why am I always at war with myself?
Why do I have to trick myself into loving
myself,
With these sentences?
They work until I falter

When can I be free,
And find the line
Between improving and
Accepting me?

Why am I still tired?
So tired of exhaustion.
Uninspired by myself;
I am nothing,
I do nothing,
I don't want to do anything.

Who wants a lover,
Like this?
Child of absence,
A boat with no engine,
Someone once told me - I do not deserve to be
loved
And I replied - yes, you are right
I am not enough,
I am not enough.

I remind myself of the methods I made
For exactly these situations
Do better, do better, do better,
do better, do better. Do. Better.
I say I love myself,
And someone whispers back:
'Why?'

How can I fix this,
So I can be worthy,
Of anything?
Or,
Am I,
Already?

////

No, I know I'm not perfect
I'm not even good,
But ill keep on trying,
Keep practising until I find new ways to think
about it,
And then one day…..
One day,
one day,
one day,
one day,
one day,
one day,
one day

Outsourced Self Worth.

In the depth of a death decided,
By a mind both feared and frightened,
On my last legs, I ran to find it,
Not hope in me, but right beside it.
To find a sense the earth was turning,
By subleasing self-love and learning -
If I kept on and fought the feeling,
If I found breath,
As an act,
Appealing,
Surely I would then become,
The ideal me you think you love.
And I would then find the place,
Where I finally,
Felt enough.

A Mantra for Universal Vibrations

I will believe, I do believe,
In the spirit, In the soul,
In vibrations of the universe,
and the connection of it all.

7AM

I haven't slept,
I say that a lot,
and It's true,
I haven't.
but also,
it's not.

I Must have slept decades,
If you add it all up,
Just not when it's needed,
too little, too much.

But, that's not important,
How have you been?
Tell me the things,
your soul have seen!

I'll be awake for two days
so,
Call any time!

Haha,
Sorry,
The fault is all mine.
I slept all weeek,
^Didn't edit that line,
Lost motivation to call you
To speak,
and bother,
to ,

try

.

Haiku

1. When my mother left
The garden grew wild and free
From sadness came life

2. I am done crying
I have cried all day, and now
there's nothing inside

3. There's an emptiness
And a pang in my stomach
Sadness or Hunger?

Monkeys Paw

When I think of nothing,
Sometimes,
I think of you.
Nothing
Reminds me of you,
I guess I got what I wanted.

Unlearning.

15

Remember when
You used to draw,
Just to see the shapes,
Your hands would make?
And you let the lies,
In your head,
..Take all that away?

- 'The worst enemy to creativity is self-doubt.' -
Sylvia Plath.

Leaving Quietly.

Days; dark
[Dis]embark
Leaving? Again?
Temporary friend.
"I miss you, my brother"
- "Message not sent."

Please, Stay Alive.

A campfire burns,
A beautiful gift,
Watching the flames,
curl, snap, and flick.

Some lashing out,
Like serpent tongues,
As kindling starts
To squeal, crack and hiss.

Now smouldering,
The fire dims,
I'll search the woods
Bring dryer sticks,
Won't let the flame give in.

Before we knew too much.

A pertinent pattern
Displayed by a [girl].
A plethora of problems,
To keep from the world.

A simmering sickness,
Burned into the [boy],
Pretends to feel nothing,
No sadness, just void.

A disparate difference,
Between the truth and the mask,
Wore scars on their sleeves,
But never their hearts.

A lifetime of lying,
They had kept on like this,
Fuelling black holes,
Self-dismissive, abyss.

An inviting ignorance,
Lies in the act,
Of losing yourself,
To feigning intact.

But, a soda shaken,
Means bubbles fizz,
A half turn, no caution?
The pressure will give.

So,
When they sat together,
Listening in silence,
Each describing,
A montage of beauty;
Speckled with violence.
There was no need,
To feign a smile.

"You're a beautiful being,"
They swapped with each other,
Both guarded, alone,
Found hope in one another.

Google Search: 'Why do I get horny when I'm trying to study?'

I masturbate to procrastinate,
And it exacerbates,
My problems,
But if I cum again,
In another ten,
Maybe then,
I'll be ready to solve them.

Mould Can Give You Asthma

In the time it took to find myself,
I drank wine bottles of my own tears,
Washed it down with a blackout,
I laughed when I fell,
I broke myself daily,
Along with some belongings,
I lived in cardboard and mould,
Until I became the mould,
Spreading darkness where I ran,
And so I ran until,
The wind blew
The mildew
From my skin,
I can still feel the spores in my chest,
But,
I don't want to rot anymore,
I drink clove oil and bleach,
Instead of my own self-pity,
And I've learned to keep moving forward,
To stop the dark patches,
Growing back.

Wait, You Don't Fuck With Weetbix & Hot Water?

I won't eat today,
Because I can't afford it,
Only have 5 Weetbix left,
I guess I could have them with hot water?
Yes, I am your friend,
And I'm somebody's daughter,
But, I really don't know who I am,

I'm like a Weetbix in hot water.

Insomnia.

Awake too late,
Happy but afraid,
That clarity is fleeting,
And I'm the only reason,
But the blame is not all on me,
I cannot fall asleep.

Amongst everything else,
I have come to accept,
This is part of myself,
My body, brain and soul,
The good, the bad,
It melds and dissolves
Into who we are.

And so in the early morning hours,
When it's well past dark
I'll harness these Insomniac powers,
Into,
What I'll call:
'Art'.

- 2018

Shutting Down: A Sexual Escapade.

\\\\\TW / SA//////

A memory,
Stolen,
Forgotten,
Lost.
Until a beckon,
To truth,
Unveils an
Unconscious loss,
Remembers,
The tremor,
The pain that's all yours,
Remembers the rape,
Remembers all four.
Now practice repeating:
What has passed,
Is gone.
Back in the room,
A lifeless,
Blank stare,
Reads cold on the outside,
You're not really there,
Just breathe,

It's okay,
No need to explain,
But, get rid of that lover,
Who sulks, cries and swears,
Your change in demeanour
Is because you don't care.

...I told you this happens.
Why are you so angry?
Why am I comforting you?

Artline 0.2mm

26

And in the end,
I'm never alone,
I always have a friend,
As long as I've got,
a paper and pen.

www.ingramcontent.com/pod-product-compliance
Lightning Source LLC
LaVergne TN
LVHW010022200726
843495LV00015B/1890